To Jeannie, Jasmine, Alex and Kathleen -
My Tribe.

Copyright © 2024 by Aaron Copeland

All rights reserved. This book or any portion thereof may not be reproduced or used in any manner whatsoever without the express written permission of the author and/or publisher except for the use of brief quotations in a book review.

Website: Inneroddballpress.com

ISBN 979-8-9908273-1-8 Hardcover
ISBN 979-8-9908273-0-1 Paperback
LCCN 2024913955

Publisher: Inneroddball Press

Editors:
  Arjuna Ardagh, Nevada City, California
  Navarre Editor Services

Our Beautiful Tribe

Written by Aaron Copeland
Illustrated by Melissa Lettis

"My beautiful Bella, are you ready for bed?" Mommy asked.

"Yes, Mommy." Bella sighed.

She picked up BB the bear and hopped in bed.

"How was your day?" Mommy asked.

"All right, I guess," Bella said.

As Mommy was tucking her in, she asked, "Bella, what's wrong? I can tell something didn't go quite right."

"Nothing, Mommy."

"Come on, Bella. You can tell me."

"I didn't get invited to Maggie's party."

In her soft assuring voice, Mommy said, "Maybe it was just very small."

"No, she invited a lot of other people. I don't think Maggie likes me anymore. We used to be special. I don't think we're special together anymore."

"Bella, you're special to so many people. You're special to your friends Dana, and Jasmine, and Jeannie. You're special to me too and loved by so many people."

"What about Daddy?"

"Daddy's away for work. But you know he loves you, don't you?"

"I guess." Bella settled BB on the pillow and remembered the bedtime story Daddy read to her the night before.

"I know Daddy loves you and misses you."

"I miss Daddy too. Good night, Daddy."

"Good night, Grandpa John and Grandma Mary."

"Grandpa and Grandma love you so much. You know that, don't you?"

"Yes, I know that."

"Grandpa Henry loves you."

"He forgot my birthday."

"He forgets a lot of things. But he still loves you. He may just not know how to say it."

"Why doesn't Grandpa Henry have a wife?"

"You never met her because she died before you were born. Her name was Louise."

"Does she love me?"

"Well, what do you think?"

Bella smiles.

"I guess she loves me too. And I guess I love her. Even though we never met."

"Did Grandpa Henry have a mommy and daddy?"

"Sure did. That was my grandma and my grandpa. They were called Martha and Edward."

"Do you think they love me too?"

"You know, Bella, I really think they do."

"Well, then I love them too."

"They are your great-grandparents."

"How many of those have I got?"

"You have eight of them. They love you, and you can love them back."

"Did they all have mommies and daddies too?"

"Yes, every single one of them had a mommy, and every single one of them had a daddy. Those mommies and daddies are your great-great-grandparents."

"Oh, my goodness, Mommy! I didn't know I had all these people. How many of those have I got?"

"You've got sixteen of them."

"That's a lot of people who love me, and a lot of people I can love back. How many people do I have altogether, if we include all the mommies of the mommies of the mommies, and the daddies of the daddies of the daddies?"

"We don't know how big the number of mommies and daddies that love you is."

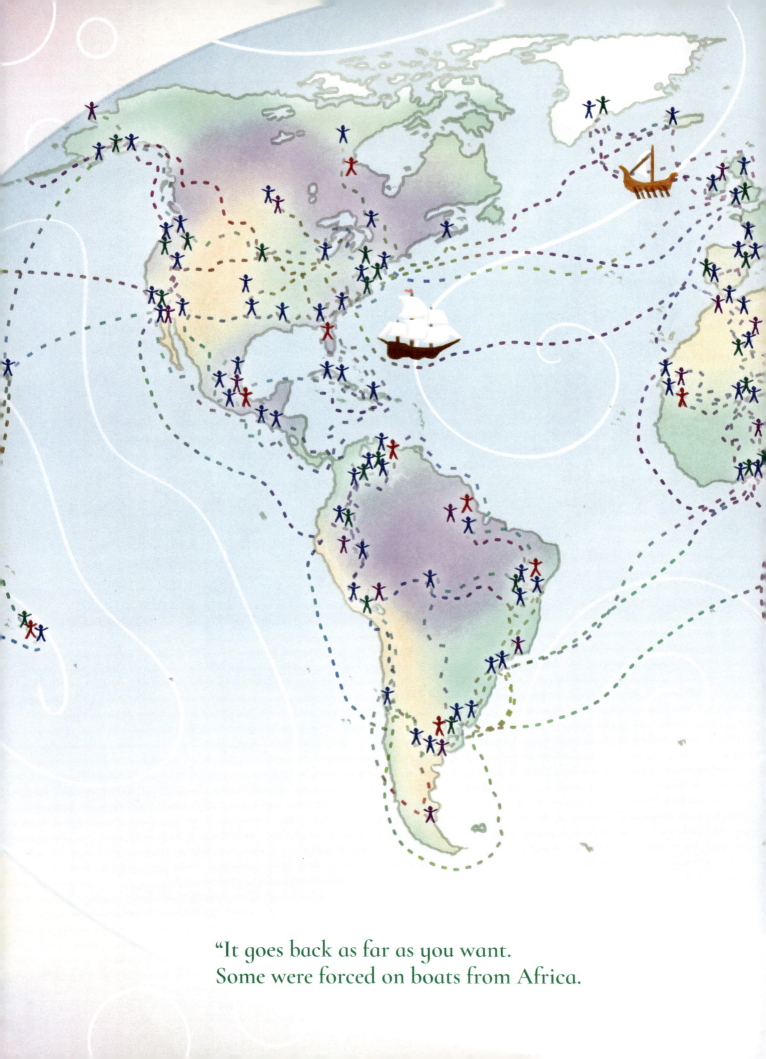

"It goes back as far as you want.
Some were forced on boats from Africa.

Some came on boats from Europe.
Some came from other places near and far."

"I didn't know about all this, Mommy. That's a lot of my people who love me, and a lot of people for me to love back."

"Maybe right now as you go to sleep, they're all watching over you, Bella, and making sure you're safe."

"I like that feeling, Mommy."

"You're special to each and every one of them.
You're special because you are their little Bella,
alive on the planet."

"Good night, all my special people. Thank you for watching over me."

"Good night, Bella."

As Bella falls asleep, the party forgotten, she knows she's loved and special to so many people.

Build Your Tribe!

Collect beautiful words from family and friends that make your child feel happy, encouraged and loved.

ABOUT THE AUTHOR

Author Aaron Copeland is a businessperson, essayist, and speaker who delves into our universal human experiences, revealing the extraordinary connections that bind us together. In his free time, Aaron enjoys spending quality moments with his wife, daughter, son and daughter in-law, and his energetic grand dog.

To see Aaron Copeland's essays visit inneroddball.com
You can reach Aaron Copeland at acopeland@inneroddball.com